AF327950

THE GOLDEN FOUNTAIN

OR

THE SOUL'S LOVE FOR GOD

BEING SOME THOUGHTS AND
CONFESSIONS OF ONE
OF HIS LOVERS

Lilian Stavley

World Wisdom Books

CURRENT EDITION 1982
WORLD WISDOM BOOKS
4211 EAST THIRD STREET
BLOOMINGTON, INDIANA 47401

The cover design is a gothic rosette.

Library of Congress Number 82-70082

How many of us inwardly feel a secret longing to find God; and this usually accompanied by the perception that we are confronted by an impenetrable barrier – we cannot find Him – we can neither go through this barrier nor climb over it! We have faith. We are able to admit that He exists, for we cannot help but perceive a Will dominating the laws of the Universe; but something deep within us that we cannot put a name to, something subtle, secret, and strange, cries aloud, 'But I need more than this, it is not enough; I need personally to find and know Him. Why does he not permit me to do so?'

We might easily answer ourselves by remembering that if, in everyday life, we greatly desire to see a friend, our best way of doing so is by going in the direction in which he is to be found: we should consider this as obvious. Then let us apply this, which we say is so obvious, to God. We waste too much time looking for Him in impossible directions and by impossible means. He is not to be found by merely studying lengthy arguments, brilliant explanations of theological statements, or controversies upon the meanings of obscure dogmas. He is not even to be found through organising charity concerts and social reforms however useful. We shall find Him through a self stripped bare of all other interests and pretensions – stripped bare of everything but a humble and passionately seeking *heart*.

He says to the soul, 'Long for Me, and I will show Myself. Desire Me with a great desire, and I will be found.'

.   .   .

Scattered all through history are innumerable persons, both great and insignificant, who looked for the Pearl of Great Price: and not too many would seem to have found it. Some sought by study, by intelligence; some by strict and pious attention to outward ceremonial service; some by a 'religious' life; some even by penance and fasting. Those who found sought with the heart. Those who sought with careful piety, or with intelligence, found perhaps faith and submission, but no joy. The Pearl is that which cannot be described in words. It is the *touch of God Himself upon the soul*, the Joy of Love.

.   .   .

The entrance to the land of happiness and peace is through union of the will to Christ, by love. How can this sense of love be reached? By centring the wheel of the mind, with its daily spinning thoughts, upon the Man-Jesus, and learning inwardly to see and hold on to the perfect simplicity and love of Jesus Christ. We can form the habit of taking Jesus as our heart and mind companion. We are all aware of the unceasing necessity of the mind to fill itself: we cannot have *no* thoughts until we have advanced in the spiritual life to a long distance. We may well see, in this, one of the provisions made by God for His own habitation in the mind of man — a habitation too often hideously usurped by every kind of unworthy substitute. Petty social interests and occupations, personal animosities, ambitions, worries, a revolving endless chaos of futilities, known and praised by too many of us as 'a busy life'! — the mind being given opportunity only at long intervals, and usually at stated and set times, to dwell upon the thought of God, and the marvellous future of the human spirit. We are like travellers who, about to start out upon a great journey, pack their portmanteaux with everything that will be *perfectly useless to them!*

Now, it is possible to put out and obliterate this chaotic and useless state of mind, which would appear to be the 'natural mind,' and to open ourselves to receive the might and force and the joys and delights of Christ's Mind. These joys are the Heart of Christ speaking to the heart of His lover. They are incomparable: beyond all imagination until we know them; and we receive them and perceive them and enjoy them as we have largeness and capacity to contain them. For there is no end. He has ever more to give if we will be but large enough to receive.

We are too absorbed in the puerile interests and occupations of daily life. We make of these endless occupations a virtue. They are no virtue, but a deadly hindrance, for they keep us too busy to look for the one thing needful – the Kingdom of God. What is this world? It is a schoolhouse for lovers, and we are lovers in the making.

Is baptism of itself sufficient to get us into this Kingdom? No. Is the leading of an orderly social life sufficient to find it? No. Is the hope, even the earnest expectation, that we shall, by some means or other (we do not know by what!), be brought to it, sufficient to find it? No; not without the *personal laying hold* can we ever achieve it. Shall we find it in much outward study? No; and our aim is, not to be the student but the possessor; and the key to this possession is not in books, but, for us, in Jesus. He it is who must be invited and admitted into the heart with great tenderness – with all those virtues for which He stands – and made the centre point of thought. Out of constant thought grows tenderness; out of tenderness, affection; out of affection, love. Love once firmly fixed in the heart for Jesus, we get a perception (by contrast) of our own faults – very painful, and known as repentance. This should be succeeded at once by change of mind, *i.e.* we try to push out the old way of thinking and acting and take on a new way. We try, in fact, strenuously to please the Beloved, to be in harmony with Him; and now we have established a personal relationship between ourselves and Christ.

With the perception of our own failings comes the necessary humility and the drastic elimination of all prides. We remember, too, that although Jesus is so near to us, and our own Beloved, He is also the mighty Son of God.

He is also the mystical Christ, who, when we are ready, leads us to the Father: which is to say, that we are suddenly stricken with the consciousness of and the love for God; and here we enter that most wonderful of all earthly experiences – the Soul's great Garden of Happiness.

To be a student of theories, dogmas, laws, and writings of men is to be involved in endless controversy; and we may study books till we are sick, and embrace nothing but vapour for all our pains. To be a pupil and possessor we must first establish the personal relationship between ourselves and Jesus. To do this we must realise more fully than we now do that He *still lives*. The mind is inclined to dwell on Him mostly as *having lived*. When we have taught ourselves to realise that Jesus is as intensely alive to everything that we do as He was when He visibly walked with men – that Jesus is as easily aware of our inmost thoughts and endeavours now as He was of the secret thoughts of His disciples, – then we shall have brought Him much closer into our own life.

As the possessor of life is not the student of schools, but is the pupil of Christ, let us prepare ourselves to be pupils; and this again we do solely by the help of the Man-Jesus, who is in Christ, and Christ in Jesus. For the Christ-God is at first too strong a meat for us: we cannot with fullness understand that He is God, but He Himself will teach us this when we are ready to know it. To know this truth in its fullness is already to possess eternal life.

As no man is able to give us eternal life, so no man is able to give us the knowledge that Christ is God, as He willed to reveal Himself to man. If we have doubts which hurt, let us drop them out, changing the thought quickly to the sweetness, simplicity, and gentleness of the Man-Jesus. If we have questionings, let us cease to question, and say with the man of old, 'Lord, I believe; help Thou mine unbelief.'

We do well to avoid these questionings, pryings, and curiosities, for when we indulge in such things we are like that common servant who does not disdain to peep through the keyhole of his master's chamber! Let us put such spiritual vulgarities upon one side, and, opening our heart to lovely Love, take Him as our only guide. Love draws us very rapidly to His own abiding-place, for we are made of love, and because of love, and for love, and to Love we must return, for He awaits us with longing.

.   .   .

We often think. Where am I at fault? I am unable to *see* myself as a sinner, though publicly I confess myself to be one. For I keep the commandments; I am friendly to my neighbours; I am just to my fellowmen; I can think of no particular harm that I do. Why, then, am I a sinner? And our very modesty and reverence may forbid us to compare ourselves with God. Yet here lies our mistake; for if we would enter the Garden of Happiness and Peace, which is the Kingdom of God, this is the commencement of our advance – that we should compare ourselves in all things with God, in whose likeness we are made, and, making such full observation as we are able of the terrible gulfs between ourselves and Him, should with tears and humility and constant endeavour be at great pains and stress to make good to Him our deficiencies.

'Be ye perfect as I am perfect.'

'Be ye holy as I am holy.'

If this were not attainable, He would not have set so high a goal. In this, then, we are sinners – that we are not pure and lovely as God Himself! This is a prodigious, an almost unthinkable, height; yet He wills us to attempt it, and all the powers of Heaven are with us as we climb.

.　　.　　.

Fear curiosity. Fear it more than sin. Curiosity is the root, and sin the flower. This is one of the reasons why we should never seek God merely with the intelligence: to do so is to seek Him, in part at least, with curiosity. God will not be peeped upon by a curious humanity. The indulgence in curiosity would of itself explain the whole downfall, so called, of man.

The Soul is the Prodigal. Curiosity *to know* led her away from the high heavens. Love is her only way of return.

Curiosity is the mother of all infidelity, whether of the spirit or of the body.

.   .   .

Though on reading the Gospels carefully we may be unable to come to any other conclusion than that Jesus Christ neither prayed for nor died for all mankind, but only for the elect, yet we see equally clearly that all mankind is *invited to be the elect*. We are, then, not individually sure of Heaven because Jesus died upon a cross for men; but sure of Heaven for ourselves only if we individually will to live and think and act in such a manner that *we become of the elect*.

'Him that cometh to Me I will in no wise cast out,' says the Voice of the Beloved.

.   .   .

In our early stages, how we shrink from the mere word, or idea, of perfection; and later, what we would give to be able to achieve it! Yet though we shrink so from the thought of it, we know instinctively that we must try to approach it; if we would stay near Him, we must be wholly pleasing to Him. We think of saints – we know nothing of saints, but think of them as most unusual persons midway between men and angels, and know ourselves not fashioned for any such position: and how change ourselves, how alter our character, as grown men and women?

It is Christ who can show us the way.

The Water of Life is the Mind of Christ, and the true object of life is to learn how to receive this Mind of Christ: for by it and with it we enter the Kingdom of God. And how shall we receive the Mind of Christ? Here is our difficulty. Firstly, we may do it through sympathy with, and a drawing near to, the Man-Jesus, accompanied by such drastic changes of mind as we are able to accomplish *to show our goodwill*. We may learn to become more unselfish, more patient, more sympathetic to others, and to curb the tongue, so that words which are untrue or unkind shall not slip off it. We can learn to govern the animal that is in us, instead of being governed by it. No one could have a better guide in how to improve the condition of his mind than Aaron Crane's book, *Right and Wrong Thinking*.

And next, having become well knitted to the Man-Jesus, the Christ will draw us forward step by step through all the next inward stages, we giving to Him our attention; and He will bring us finally to that marvellous condition of God-consciousness by which He is able perpetually to refresh and renew us. There is one great first rule to hold to, which is *to think lovingly of Jesus*: in this way we eventually and automatically *come into a state of love*. In which state He will teach us to put out our own little light, that we may learn to live by the lovely light of God. And we have entered the Kingdom!

For myself, I experienced three conversions: the first two of terrible suffering, and the third of great and marvellous joy, in which it is no exaggeration to say that for a few moments I seemed to receive God and all the freedom of the Heavens into my soul. I am not able to say exactly how long this experience lasted, for I was dead to time and place, but I should judge it to have been from fifteen to twenty minutes.

The first conversion came upon me one afternoon in my room, as I came in from walking. I had been thinking of Jesus while I walked, as I was often in the habit of doing. Without any intention or premeditation on my part, I was now suddenly overwhelmed by a most horrible, unbearable, inexplicable pain of remorse for my vileness: for I seemed suddenly to be aware of Him standing there in His marvellous purity and looking at me – not with any reproach, but with the sweetness of a wonderful Invitation upon His face. And immediately I saw myself utterly unworthy to come near Him: and I writhed in the agony of this fearful perception of my unworthiness till I could bear no more. I was sick and ill with remorse and regret, I was utterly broken up by it. I did not know then that this awful pain is what is known as repentance, and wondered secretly what could have come to me. After this I found myself far more constantly thinking of

Jesus – exchanging, as it were, sweet confidences with Him, telling Him what I thought, and endeavouring in every possible way to follow His manner of thought. I am ashamed to say I was very remiss and lazy in prayers; upon my knees I prayed very little indeed. But I was very faithful and warm and tender to Him in my heart, and this had an effect upon my mind and actions, and continued for two years.

I would be assailed by many questionings during this time. For instance, how could my sweet Jesus, whom I was always so near to, be the mighty Christ and God? But I dropped these out as they came, feeling myself altogether too small to understand these things, and very much frightened by such greatnesses.

When I was alone with Jesus, all was so simple and so lovely; so I put away all other thoughts and held closely to Jesus.

This having continued almost exactly the two years, upon Easter morning, at the close of the service, the horrible anguish came on me again as I knelt in the church. I was not able to move or to show my face for more than an hour; and to this day I am not able to dwell upon the memory of that awful pain, for I think I should go mad if I had to enter again into so great a torture of the spirit. I endured to the utmost limit of my capacity for suffering – for this I will say of myself, I did not draw back, but went on to the bitter end. And the suffering was caused by the sight of that most terrible of all sights: the vision of myself as over against the vision of Jesus Christ, and I died a death for every fault. Whoever has felt the true wailing of the soul, such an one knows the heights of all spiritual pain. The heart and mind, or creature, suffers in depths; but the soul in heights, and this at one and the same time, so that the pain of repentance is everywhere. And the depth of the suffering of the creature is coequal with the height of the suffering of the soul, and the joint suffering of both would seem to be of coequal promise and merit for their after joy and glory; so that it would seem that the more horrible our pain, the quicker is our deliverance and the greater our later joys.

After this, Jesus, without my knowing how it came about, passed out from the Perfect Man into the Christ of God. I walked and talked with Him no longer just as sweet Jesus, but as the Marvellous and Mighty Risen Lord! And now I became far more changed. The world and all earthly loves began to fade; they no longer satisfied or filled me in the least. How could I contemplate His exquisite perfections, the ineffable beauties of His mind and heart, and, turning from these to the sight of the world and of the men and women that I knew, not feel the difference? Where among my friends could I find perfect love? Amongst husbands and wives? No. Amongst mothers and children? No. For everywhere I saw discord, secret selfishness, separate and divided desires, and many deceits. I found no love anywhere like His for us. I was always an epicure in the matter of love, and knew the best when I found it. I continued with my social and home life exactly as before: the change was an inward change.

Almost immediately after this the War came, and, with it, torments of anxiety over my earthly loves.

The fearful anxiety I was in drove me to prayer. I began to pray more regularly; but though I prayed, I remained as miserable as before. A painful illness came, and lasted four months. I had no home because of the War, and nowhere to be ill in peace: and I drank and ate wretchedness as my daily bread and wine, and wondered why I ever was born.

I cannot recall I was ever rebellious, No, I never was. I walked in a maze of trouble, and endured like a poor dumb thing, *and did not throw out my heart to God enough* in prayer. If I had done this I think I should have been through my pains in half the time.

Two years went by, and, being in greater anxiety than ever because of a great battle that was going on and my love at the front of it, I went up on the hill where I often went, and standing there I contended with God, crying out, 'It is too much – the pain of this war is too great and too long; I cannot bear it, I am at an end of everything. Help me! Help me!' And in my anguish I seemed at last to be melted and running like water before Him, and I came before Him as it were immediately before a mighty and living Presence, though I saw nothing.

But though I was so near Him and appealed to Him with the whole of my strength, there was no answer, no reply, but the great silence of Heaven.

At last, my agony over, I walked for a little, very quiet and very sad, and all at once a marvellous thing happened to me. I will not here describe how it was done to me, but He filled me with love for Himself, an amazing, all-absorbing, and tremendous love – from the crown of my head to the soles of my feet I was filled with love. And this was His answer – and all my sorrows fled away in a great joy.

This third conversion produced a fundamental alteration of my whole outlook and grasp on life. It brought me into direct contact with God, and was the commencement of a total change of heart and mind and consciousness; the centre of my consciousness, without any effort of my own, suddenly moving bodily from a concentration upon the visible or earthly to a loving and absorbed concentration upon, and a fixed attention to, the Invisible God – a most amazing, undreamed-of change, which remained permanent, though fluctuating through innumerable degrees of intensity before coming to a state of equilibrium. And now Christ went away from me, so that I adored Him in God. After this for some weeks I went through extraordinary spiritual experiences, the like of which had never previously so much as entered into my heart to imagine; again I will say nothing here of these. I came to all these experiences with great innocence and ignorance, never having read any religious or psychological book, and I think now that it is perhaps easier to have it so.

Knowing that nothing is done without a purpose, I would question myself what I could possibly be intended to learn out of these things; and though I have never yet found a reason for any one given experience, yet I see this: the whole (which lasted for some weeks and was gone through at night and always in a state of semi-wakefulness, for the body would be stiff and set like a board) – the whole was the most convincing proof that He could have given me (without destroying my flesh) of the reality of the life unseen. For how otherwise could we be made to know of the reality of spiritual things if we were never *taken into* them? And having been taken into them, and they being a thousand times more poignant than any earthly experience, how could we forget them? Whenever doubts upon anything presented themselves, I had nothing more to do than to Remember! Nothing He could have devised to do for me could have been of greater or more direct assistance to me. These experiences were to my creature what the centre-board is to the racing yacht. With these memories I could keep an even keel, and without them I must have capsized many a time.

By these spiritual experiences He gives us an immense courage, and personal knowledge of a mysterious and hitherto unknown life of joys so great and so intense that all sufferings endured by us here appear to us in their true light as being a melting and cleansing agency infinitely worth while, that we may gain in permanence such exquisite felicity.

Our means of reaching a personal experience, whilst still in the body, of such a life of joys is to harmonise the spirit of our human creature to the degree of purity required by the soul to enable her in unfettered freedom to perform her divine functions.

We confuse in our minds the two separate essences – that of the soul and that of the human spirit (heart, intelligence, and will), which are widely different; the soul acting for us as the wings of the creature. And above and superior to the soul, and yet within it, is the divine and incorruptible Spirit or Sparkle of God, which in its turn acts as the wings of the soul. So we have the worm (or creature-spirit), the soul; and the Celestial Spark, or Divine Intelligence of the soul, which is the organ of God, and with which we are able to come in *sensible contact* with the divine world and God Himself. What are our enemies? Selfishness, impatience, covetousness, pride, ill-temper, bodily indulgences, and, above all, indifference to God of the will of the creature.

After this third, and last, conversion upon the hill, which so altered my whole life, I was for a period of some months in such a state of exaltation and enhancement of all my faculties that I did not know myself at all. I was, without any intention or endeavour on my own part, suddenly become like a veritable House of Arts! The most beautiful music flowed through my mind, in which I noticed certain peculiarities – there was no sadness in it, and it swayed me so that I seemed to go into a state of white heat with emotion over it. It was extraordinarily much smoother than any earth-music I ever heard, and extremely consecutive, like a fluid. Now with earth-music I find that even Wagner is not able to achieve any consecutive perfection: he reaches to a height – only to fall back and disappoint. But this other music, which is not heard with the senses but is invariably felt by the soul, remains at extreme and fluid perfection, and casts such spells over the listener that he is beside himself with enjoyment. Colour and form, imagery of all kinds, would pass through me till I felt like an artist, and cried out with regret, 'Oh, if I had only studied this or that art and knew the grounding of it, what heights of proficiency I could reach now!' An object of quite ordinary charm seemed, because of that something which now filled me, to expand into prodigious beauty! The very pavements and houses, mean and hideous as they are, overflowed with some inexplicable glamour. The world was turned into a veritable paradise! When I thought of it all I was filled with amazement, and still am, for how can we explain such changes in manner of living and seeing? At this time my only trouble or difficulty was to conceal my condition from others.

But this wonderful state of things gradually passed away, and I went into a most difficult condition. At one time of the day I would be in an ecstasy of delight, and an hour later in some altogether unreasonable depth of wretchedness. I went to and fro from one extreme to the other, and my time was, I think, mostly spent in trying to regain some kind of balance.

My love for God was as great as ever, but it had become a love all made of tears. Indeed, my whole being seemed made of tears. I thought often of these words, the peace of God; most certainly I had not found it. On the contrary, my life had become an indescribable turmoil. I found no help from my fellow-beings; I seemed to have lost the power of talking pleasantly with them, and my point of view had become different from theirs. Men could no longer please me, and I could not please God! I was entirely alone spiritually, and I said to myself it would be better if I could be alone physically as well; and I ached and longed and dreamed of solitude till it was like a sickness. But the only solitude I could have was in my own room.

Now, believing myself to be a sensible and practical person, I would say to myself that my condition, being so unreasonable, must be got out of, and I must make every effort to do it. I prayed for two things – that I might love God with a cheerful countenance and not with tears, and that He would teach me quickly what to pray for; and He gave me the impulse to pray for more and greater love.

Next, I banished my own feelings as much as I could (since love must not think of itself), paying as little attention to them as possible by perpetually dropping them out as they came and returning to the thought of Jesus, concerning myself at all times of the day to living inward conversation with Him; and in this manner I fastened myself closer than ever to Him, continually praying for greater love to give Him and passionately offering Him all that I already had, whilst with all my will and strength I tried to climb out of my miserable state. Soon I succeeded – I was out of it in a matter of weeks.

. . .

How humanity is extolled by its own kind! How men are admired, even glorified! I am amazed, for where is the glory of any man? But rather, how wonderful and glorious is God, that He should cause to spring from one handful of dust such possibilities! Wonderful God! And blessed man, that he should have so wonderful a God!

Some men say that man has invented for himself the thought of God, because of the great need he feels within himself for such a being.

Yet look where we will in Nature, do we find a warrant for such a thought? Are babes inspired with the desire for milk, and is that milk withheld from the nature of all mothers? No; to the babe is given the desire because the mother has wherewith to satisfy. So with grown men: for to us is given a deep and secret desire for the milk of God's love, and to Himself He has reserved the joy of leading us to it and bestowing it upon us.

.   .   .

Sometimes for a short while the soul will suffer from a sickness (I speak now for persons already very well advanced); she is parched and without sweetness. Her love has no joy in it. This is not a condition to be accepted or acquiesced in, but must be overcome at once by a remedy of prayer: prayer addressed to the Father, *in the name of Jesus Christ*, a prayer of praise and adoration – 'I praise and bless and love and thank Thee, I praise and bless and love and worship Thee, I praise and bless and love and glorify Thee' – till the heart is fired and we return to the intimacy of love. Or the Lord's Prayer, very slow, and with an intention both outgoing and *intaking*. So far I have never known these remedies to fail, and joy floods the soul and sends her swinging up, up on to the topmost heights again. It is magnificent.

How is it that we can pass so, up from the visible into the Invisible, and become so one with it, and feel it so powerfully, that the Invisible becomes a thousand times more real to us than the visible! It is like a different manner of living altogether. And when anyone so living finds himself even for a short time unfastened from this way of living and back again to what is known to the average as normal life, this normal life seems no better to him than some horrible chaotic and uneven turmoil, and his brain ready to be turned if he had to remain in it for long. When so unfastened, the whole savour of life is completely gone, and a smallness of mind and outlook is fallen back into, from which the soul recoils in horror and struggles quickly to free herself.

Is this the remnant of the unruly creature rising up and grappling with the soul again? Is this some deliberate trial of us by the Master? – or some natural spiritual sickness? Whilst in this condition we must disappoint the Beloved. On the other hand, we find ourselves kept to the knowledge of our own impotence and nothingness and dependence, and the spirit is strengthened by the efforts made quickly to recover the lost beautiful estate.

Also we become more able to feel true patience and compassion for such others as do not know the way of escape. So we gain, maybe, more than we lose.

. . .

We may wonder how it is that the Mighty Maker of the Universe should choose to condescend to the mere individual piece of clay. It is incomprehensible. It is so incomprehensible that there is but one way of looking at it. This is no favouritism to the individual, but the evidence of a Mind with a vast plan pursuing a way and using a likely individual. These individuals or willing souls He takes and, setting them apart, fashions them to His own ends and liking. Of one He will make a worker, and of another He fashions to Himself a lover. It would seem to be His will to use the human implement to help the human. As water, for usefulness to the many, must be collected and put through channels, so it would seem must the beneficence of God be collected into human vessels and channels that it may be distributed for the use of the many and the more feeble.

.   .   .

The more any man will consider humanity, the more he will see that the education of the heart and will is of more importance than the education of the brain. For in the perfectly trained and educated heart and will we find the evidence of highest wisdom.

.   .   .

Why mortify the body with harsh austerities? When we over-mortify the body with fastings, pains, and penances we are *remembering the flesh*.

Let us aim at the forgetting and not the despising of the flesh. A sick body can be a great hindrance to the soul. By keeping the body in a state of perfect wholesomeness we can more easily pass away from the recollection of it. Chastise the mind rather than the body. Christ taught, not the contempt or wilful neglect of the body, but the humble submission of the body to all *circumstances*, the obedience of the will to God, and the glorious and immeasurable possibilities of the human spirit.

.   .   .

We know that the love of the heart can be beautiful and full of zeal and fervour; but the love of the soul by comparison to it is like a furnace, and the capacities of the heart are not worthy to be named in the same breath. Yet, deplorable as is the heart of man, it is evidently desired by God, and must be given to Him before He will waken the soul. To my belief, we are quite unable to awaken our own soul, though we are able to *will* to love God with the heart, and through this we pass up to the border of the Veil of Separation, where He will *sting the soul into life* and we have Perception.

After which the soul will often be swept or plucked up into immeasurable glories and delights which are neither imagined nor contrived, nor even desired by her at first — for how can we desire that which we have never heard of and cannot even imagine? And these delights are unimaginable before the soul is caught up into them, and to my experience they constantly differ. The soul knows herself to be in the hands and the power of another, outside herself. She does not enter these joys of her own power or of her own will, but by permission and intention and will of a force outside herself though perceived and known inside herself. No lovers of arguments or guessing games can move the soul to listen when she has once been so handled. For to know is more than to guess.

.　　.　　.

How can a Contact with God be in any way described? It is not seeing, but meeting and fusion with awareness. The soul retaining her own individuality and consciousness to an intense degree, but imbued with and fused into a life of incredible intensity, which passes through the soul vitalities and emotions of a life so new, so vivid, so amazing, that she knows not whether she has been embraced by love or by fire, by joy or by anguish: for so fearful is her joy that she is almost unable to endure the might of it.

And how can the heat or fire of God be described? It is very far from being like the cruelty of fire, and yet it is so tremendous that the mind knows of little else to compare it to. But it is like a vibration of great speed and heat, like a fluid and magnetic heat.

This heat is of many degrees and of several

kinds. The heat of Christ is mixed with indescribable sweetness: giving marvellous pleasure and refreshment and happiness, and wonderfully adapted to the delicacy of the human creature. The heat of the Godhead is very different, and sometimes we may even feel it to be cruel and remorseless in its very terrible and swift intensity. But the soul, like all great lovers, never flinches or hangs back, but passionately lends herself. If He chose to kill her with this joy she would gladly have it so.

By these incomprehensible wonders He seems to say to the creature: 'Come thou here, that I may teach thee what is Joy; come thou here, that I may teach thee what is *Life*. For none is permitted to teach of these things save I Myself.'

.   .   .

There is another manner. The Spirit comes upon the soul in waves of terrible power. Now in a rapture God descends upon the soul, catching her suddenly up in a marvellous embrace: magnetising her, ravishing her. He is come, and He is gone. In an ecstasy the soul goes out prepared to meet Him, seeking Him by praise and prayer, pouring up her love towards Him; and He, condescending to her, fills her with unspeakable delights, and at rare times He will catch her from an ecstasy into a greater rapture. At least, so it is with me: the ecstasy is prepared for, but in the quicker rapture (or catching up) it is He that seeks the soul. These two conditions, though given very intermittently, become a completely natural experience. I should say that the soul lived by this way: it is her food and her life, which she receives with all the simplicity and naturalness of the hungry man turning to his bodily food. But these waves of power were something altogether new and very hard to endure. As each wave passed I would come up out of it, as it were, gasping. It was as if something too great for the soul to contain was being forced through her. It was as if one should try to force at fearful pressure fluid through a body too solid to be percolated by it. I understood nothing of what could be intended by such happenings, neither could I give accommodation to this intensity. I tried to make myself a wholly willing receptacle and instrument, but after the third day of this I could not bear any more. I was greatly distressed. I could not understand what was required of me. I gave myself totally to Him, and it was not enough. And at last I cried to Him, saying: 'I understand nothing: forgive me, my God, for my great foolishness, but Thy power is too much for me. Do what Thou wilt with me; I am altogether Thine. Drown me with Thy strength, break me in pieces – I am willing; only do it quickly, my Lord, and have done with it, for I am so small. But I love Thee with all that I have or am; yet I am overwhelmed: I am still too little to be taught in this way, it is too much for my strength. Yet do as Thou wilt;

I love Thee, I love Thee.' And He heard me, and He ceased: and He returned to the ways that I understood and dearly loved, and for weeks I lived in Paradise. But my body was dreadfully shaken, and I suffered with my heart and breathing.

Shortly after I began to know that another change had come into me. God had become intensely my Father, and Christ the lover was gone up again into the Godhead – as happened after my third conversion upon the hill.

So great, so tremendous was this sense of the *Fatherhood* of God become that I had only to think the word Father to seem to be instantly transported into His very bosom. Oh, the mighty sweetness of it! But it is not an ecstasy. The creature and soul are dead to world-life, as in a rapture or ecstasy; but the soul is not the bride, she is the child, and, full of eager and adoring intimacy, she flies into His ever-open arms, and never, never does she miss the way. Oh, the sweetness of it, the great, great glory of it, and the folly of words! If only all the world of men and women could have this joy! How to help even one soul towards it is what fills my heart and mind. How convince them, how induce them to take the first steps? It is the first steps we need to take. He does not drive, He calls. 'Come to Me,' He calls. It is this failure to have the will to go to Him which is the root of all human woe. Would we but take the first few steps towards Him, He will carry us all the rest of the way. These first few steps we take holding to the hand of Jesus. For the so-called Christian there is no other way (but he is no Christian until he has taken it). For the Buddhist, doubtless, Gautama is permitted to do the same. But for those who are baptised in Jesus Christ's name, He is their only Way.

.   .   .

God, once found, is so poignantly ever-present to the soul that we must sing and whisper to Him all the day.

O marvellous and exquisite God! I am so enraptured by Thy nearness, I am so filled with love and joy, that there is no one, nothing, in heaven or earth to me save Thine Own Self, and I could die for love of Thee! Indeed I am in deep necessity to find Thee at each moment of the day, for so great is Thy glamour that without Thee my days are like bitter waters and a mouthful of gravel to a hungry man. How long wilt Thou leave me here – set down upon the earth in this martyrdom of languishing for love of Thee? And suddenly, when the pain can be endured no more, He embraces the soul. Then where do sorrow and waiting fly? – and what is pain? There never were such things!

.   .   .

We do well never to recall past ecstasies. In this way the soul comes to each encounter with a lovely freshness and purity, and neither makes comparisons nor curious comments, but gives herself wholly to love. But by these contacts the soul gains a secret and personal knowledge of God: without sight and without reasoning she actually feels to partake of God, so that she passes by these means far up beyond belief, into experiences of knowledge which in their poignant intensity are at once an ineffable violence and a marvellous white peace.

. . .

I find the lark the most wonderful of all birds. I cannot listen to his rhapsodies without being inspired (no matter what I may be in the midst of doing or saying) to throw up my own love to God. In the soaring insistence of his song and passion I find the only thing in Nature which so suggests the high-soaring and rapturous flights of the soul. But I am glad that we surpass the lark in sustaining a far more lengthy and wonderful flight; and that we sing, not downwards to an earthly love, but upwards to a heavenly.

To my mind, this is man's only justification for considering himself above the beasts – that we can love, and communicate with, God. For where otherwise is his superiority? He builds fine buildings which crumble and decay. He digs holes in the earth to take out treasures which he has not made; and if he makes himself the very highest tower of wealth or fame, he must come down from it and be buried in the earth like any other carcase.

* * *

It is better not to contend, either with others or against our own body. If we contend against anything we impress it the more firmly upon our consciousness. So if we would overcome the lusts of the body, let us do it not by harming or by contending against the body, which but emphasises its powers and importance, but let us rather proceed to ignore and make little of the body by forgetting it and passing out of it into higher things; and eventually we shall learn to live, not in the lower state, but in the joy of the soul. Why have a contempt for the body? I once did, and found that I was committing a great sin against the Maker of it.

How dare we say 'my body is vile,' when He fashioned it! It is blasphemous, when we consider that it is His Temple.

To my mind the body is a beautiful and wonderful thing, and is greatly sinned against by our evil hearts and minds and tongues. The body would do no harm if we, with our free-will, did not think out the wickedness first in our own hearts. For first we commit theft and adultery with the mind, and then we cause the body to carry out these things. We know that the body is under the law, and its appetites are under the law, but the heart and mind and tongue are perpetual breakers of this law. It is lawful for the body to take its meat and drink, but not to be surfeited and drunken. It is lawful for the body to have its desires and its loves, but not to be promiscuous and unfaithful.

But we know that a better way is to turn all appetites and greeds to this; that we be greedy and ravenous for Christ. Only so shall we use the appetites of mind and heart and body for their true end, and that not by despising but by conversion.

With great insistence I have been taught not to despise anything whatever in Creation of *things made* in His most beautiful and wonderful world, though often I may cry with tears, 'Lord God! raise me to a world holier and nearer to Thyself, for I am heartbroken here.'

Yet I am taught only to despise such things as lying, deceitfulness, hypocrisy, and uncleanness – in fact, stenches of the heart and mind, – and not to think too much about these, but, passing on, drop out the recollection of them in thoughts of finer things.

His inward instruction has been this, quietly to lay upon one side all that which is not pleasing to God; and one by one, and piece by piece, to fold up and put away all that He does not love.

Above all, He has taught me to have no self-esteem and no prides; and to such a degree do I have to learn this, that, without the smallest exaggeration, I am hardly ever able to think myself the equal of a dog. But the love of a dog for his master is a very fine thing.

.   .   .

I think we mistake our own power and capacity in even seeking to imitate the Christ; let us begin rather by taking into our heart and our mind the Christ as the Man-Jesus. For His love and power only can show us the way to imitate the Christ which is in Him.

.   .   .

Is the temporary loss of grace our fault, or is it a deliberate withdrawal and testing upon His part? Both. Every condition that we are in which is not pure and perfect of its kind, such as pure peace, pure joy, pure harmony, is because of failure on our part to *hold* to Him. Whenever, and for so long, as we keep ourselves in the single and simple condition of mind and heart necessary for the perception and reception of Him, for just so long shall we receive and perceive him; but this condition again we cannot maintain without grace. All loss of joy, of serenity, of contact, is failure, then, on our part or withdrawal upon His. Yet we learn a bitter but useful lesson by these losses of ability for connection. To return ignominiously to our dust is a most bitter humiliation and trial — indeed, a desolation. Now, if we did not so return we might suppose ourselves able, of our own power, not only to achieve momentary connection with the Divine, but to remain at will in this sublime condition, by which I mean in a state bordering upon ecstasy. The withdrawal of grace therefore would seem to be a necessary part of the education and of the constant humbling of the soul. To find ourselves, of our own unaided capacity, by the mere force of our own will, able constantly to go up to so high a level would inevitably foster pride; indeed, to attain such a capacity would seem to place us on a level with the angels!

By these withdrawals of grace, which came at first very tenderly, but gradually with greater and greater severity, I have learnt this: that in spite of all that has been done for me, of all that I have experienced, in spite of all the heights to which at times I have been raised, I remain nothing better than the frailest and unworthiest thing! The sight of an ugly grey cloud, momentarily and gloriously illumined by the sun, is a sufficient illustration of the temporary transformation of our own selves touched by the light and the glory of God.

For the carrying out of His plan, it would seem to be His good pleasure that we are just what we are – not angels, but little human things, full of simplicity and trust and love. 'Like dear children,' as St Paul says; and yet, oh! wonder of wonders! *far more than this*. For whilst we patiently wait, from time to time He stoops and embraces the soul in an infinite bliss, in which we are no more children, but are caught up into High Love.

At first when we begin this new kind of living He holds us firmly, as it were, to a condition suitable for contact with Him. If He did not do so, having had no previous practice, we should never remain in it for two moments together. Then little by little He teaches us to live with less frequent joy, and this is the cause of much difficulty and trouble. It is hard to endure being without this blessed state and these marvellous favours, and more and more I found He withdrew them whilst often my worldly and commonplace heart and mind still held me back – *even from peace*. If we could but rid ourselves quickly of all selfish desires and greeds! Not until I had learnt to do this was I given back my joys, and then sparingly.

How I would turn towards that secret door – the door of the kingdom of love – and calling to Him, hear no reply! Where is He gone? – why this desertion? – I would cry. How can He cause such pain, how can I bear such dreadful deprivations, and what is love but a sharp sword? Lord let me hear Thy voice, for I am in despair; I cannot bear these pains, I fear for everything, my joy is lost. My bread is spread with bitterness; where is the honey that I love so well? Lord, call to me even from far away, and I shall hear and be consoled. Lord, I am sick and ill – how canst Thou leave me so? Hast Thou no pity for my pain? – is this Thy love? *My* pain! Lord, I remember! Thou hast been kissed by pain more frequently than I.

Oh, let me wipe the memory of Thy pain away with my warm love, and let me sing to Thee and be Thy lark, and do Thou go and wander where Thou wilt and I will love Thee just the same! And softly the Voice of the Beloved, saying: 'I am here, I never left thee; but thou wast busy crying of thy pains and did not hear Me when I answered thee.' Lord, so I was! I was so filled with self, and, asking for *Thy gifts, I did forget to give* and so lost love.

It is hard to conquer in small things, petty irritations, worries, cares of this world, likes and dislikes -- all of these being subtle temptations, and all selfish. For instance, very often I find the human voice the most horrible thing that I know! I will be in a beautiful state of mind, and people around me will drag me from it with their maddening inanities of conversation. This one will speak of the weather, and that one of food; another of scandal, another of amusements. They will talk of their love for a dog, for a horse, for golf, for men or women; but never do I hear at any time, or anywhere, anyone speak of their love for God. I must listen to all their loves, but if I should venture to speak of mine they would look at me amazed; indeed, I never should dare to do it. And this is perhaps the greatest weakness that I have to fight against now, and one that spoils the harmony of the mind more than any other – that I cannot always control myself from secret though unspoken irritation, impatience, and criticisms; and to criticise is to judge, and in this there is wrong, and the smallest breeze of wrong is enough to blow-to – even to close – the door into that other lovely world. And not only this, but every such failure is a disappointment to the Beloved. Many times I say to Him, 'What canst Thou do with us all, Beloved – such a mass of selfish, foolish, blundering, sinful creatures, all hanging and pulling on to Thee at the same moment?' And I will be filled with a passionate desire to so progress that I may stand a little alone and not be a perpetual drag upon Him, and, feeling strong, perhaps I will say: 'I will give up my share of Thee to someone else, and not draw upon Thee for a little while, my Beloved Lord.' But oh, in less than an hour, if He should take me at my word! I could cry and moan like a small child, in my horrible emptiness and longing for Him. And where now is my strength? – I have not an ounce of it without Him! By this I learn in my own person how He is life itself to us, in all ways. He is the air, the bread, and the blood of the soul, and no one can live without at every moment drawing upon Him, though they do it insensibly. What a weight to carry, what a burden, this whole hungry clamouring mass of disobedient men and women! Oh, my Beloved, how frequently I weep for all Thy bitter disappointment – never ending!

But this we may be sure of – that all the marvels

of His grace are not poured out on some poor scrappit for no other reason than to give him pleasure. There is a vast purpose behind it all, and by keenest attention we must pick up this purpose, understand it, *and do it*. This is the true work of man, to love God with all the heart and mind and soul and strength, and not those material works with which we all so easily satisfy ourselves and our consciences, and our *bodily* needs.

He has marvellous ways (and very difficult to the beginner) of conveying His wishes. To my finding, the inward life of us is like a perpetual interchange of conversation between the heart and its many desires and the mind (which for myself I put into three parts – the intelligence, the will, the reason). Now, all these parts of my heart and of my mind formerly occupied themselves entirely with worldly things, passing from one thing to another in most disorderly fashion; but now they occupy themselves (save for bodily necessities) *solely* with Him. There is a perpetual smooth and beautiful conversation between them *to* Him and *of* Him; and suddenly He will seem to enter into this conversation, suggesting thoughts which are not mine.

Often He will stab the soul, but not with words, also the heart; and I have known such communications lie for weeks before they could be taken up by the mind, turned into words, and finally as *words* be digested by the reason. And another way to the soul only – rare, untransferable to words, and therefore not transmittable to others or to the reason. This way causes the creature a great amazement, and is like a flooding or moving of whiteness, or an inwardly-felt phosphorescence; it is a vitalising ministration greatly enjoyed by the soul. This is not any ecstasy, and is exceedingly swift; the soul must be at *high attention* to receive this, yet neither anticipates nor asks for it, but is in the act of giving great and joyful adoration.

      ·   ·   ·

I do not remember when I first became fully conscious that the centre or seat of my emotions was changed, and that I now responded to all the experiences of life only with the higher parts of me.

This change I found inexplicable and remarkable, for it was fundamental, and yet neither intended nor thought of by me. With this alteration in the physical correspondences to life came a corresponding alteration in the spiritual part of me.

Formerly I supposed that the soul dwelt in, or was even a part of, the mind. Now, though the mind must be filled wholly with God, and all other things whatsoever put out of it if we would contemplate Him or respond to Him, yet neither the brain nor the intelligence of the creature can come into any contact with Him; and this I soon learnt.

Correspondence with the Divine is accomplished for the creature through the heart and by the uppermost part of the breast, this latter place (above the heart and below the mind) is the dwelling-place of the celestial spark of the soul, which lies, as it were, between two fires – that of the heart and that of the mind, responding directly to neither of these, but to God only.

Before I was touched upon the hill I was not aware of the locality of any part of my soul, neither was there anything which could convince me that I even possessed a soul. I did no more than believe and suppose that I did possess one. But the soul, once revived, becomes the most powerful and vivid part of our being; we are not able any longer to mistake its possession or position in the body. She is indeed the wonderful and lovely mistress of us, with which alone we can unlock the mysteries of God's love.

·　　·　　·

How poor and cold a thing is mere belief! No longer do I *believe* in Jesus Christ: I do *possess him*. So complete is the change that He brings about in us that I now only count my life and my time from the first day of this new God-consciousness that I received upon the hill, for that was the first day of my real life; just as formerly I would count my time from the first day of my physical birth, and from that on to my falling in love and to my marriage, which once seemed to me to be the most important dates.

Whilst these changes were taking place in me I would often be filled with uneasiness and some alarm; asking myself what all this could mean and if it could be the way of martyrs or saints, for I had no courage or liking to be one or the other and was very frightened of suffering. And I think my cunning heart would have liked to take all the sweets and leave the bitter. How well He knew this, and how exquisitely He handled me, never forcing, only looking at me, *inviting* me with those marvellous perfections of His! How could I possibly resist Him? All the while, all my waking hours, I felt that strange, new, incomprehensible, steady, insistent *drawing* and urgency of the Spirit in me. Little by little I went – and still go – *towards* perfection, whilst my cowardly heart endured many fears, but these are now past. It was not any desire for my own salvation; to this I have never given so much as two thoughts. It was the *irresistible attraction* of our marvellous and beautiful God. He lured, He drew me with His loveliness, His holy perfections, His unutterable purity. *I longed to please Him.* The whole earth was filled with the glamour of Him, and I filled with horror to see how utterly unlike – apart from the glorious Beloved – I was. How frightful my blemishes, which must stink in His nostrils! Think of it! To stink in the nostrils of the Beloved! What lover could endure to do such a thing? No effort could be too great or painful to beautify oneself for Him. In this there is no virtue; it is the driving necessity of love, a necessity known by every lover worthy of the name on earth. To please and obey this ineffable and exquisite Being! – the privilege intoxicated me more and more.

All these changes in my heart and mind continually filled me with surprise, for I was never pious, though inwardly and secretly I had so ardently sought Him. I was attentive, humble, and reverent, nothing more.

But though I had perhaps little or no piety, and never read a single religious book, I had had a deep thirst for the perfect and the holy and the pure, as I seemed unable to find them here on the earth. In the quiet solemnity of church, or under the blue skies, I could detach myself from my surroundings and reach up and out with wistful dimness towards the ineffable holiness and purity of God – God who, for me at least, remained persistently so unattainable.

And yet one blessed day I was to find Him suddenly, all in one glorious hour, no longer unattainable but immanently, marvellously near, and willing to remain for me so strangely permanently near that I must sing silently to Him from my heart all the day long – sing to Him silently, because even the faintest whisper would feel too gross and loud between my soul and Him. And in hours when I fall from this wonderful estate I think I come very near hell, so awful is my loss.

Our greatest need is to relearn the will of God. For we are so separated from Him that we now look upon His Will as on a cross, as an incomprehensible sacrifice, as but self abnegation, pain, and gloom. We repudiate it in terror.

If we have the will to relearn His Will, we stand still and think of it, we walk to seek it, we try to accept it, trembling we bow down to it with obedience and many tears; and behold! it changes to an Invitation, a sigh of beauty, a breath of spring, the song of birds, the faces of flowers, the ever-ascending spiral of the mating of all loves, the sunshine of the Universe; and at last, intoxicated with happiness, we say: 'My God, my Love, I sip and drink Thy Will as an ambrosial Wine!'

    .   .   .

To the lover of God all affections go up and become enclosed, as it were, into one affection which is Himself; so that we have no love for anyone or anything *apart* from Him. In this is included, in a most deep and mysterious fashion, marriage-love in all its aspects. In every way it can become a sacrament: there is nothing in it which is not holy, in no way does the marriage bond of the body separate the spirit from acceptableness to God.

But I was some time before I could arrive at this, and could see marriage as the physical prototype in this physical world of the spiritual union with Himself in the spiritual world. And this was arrived at, not by prudish questionings and criticisms, but by remembering that this relationship between men and women is His thought, His plan, not ours. We are responsible for our part in it only in so far as to keep the bond of it pure and clean and sweet, and submit ourselves in all things *as completely and orderly as possible to His plans, whatever they may be.* In this attitude of *un*questioning, *un*resisting submission, the Holy Spirit finds a swift and easy channel through us. It is our opposition to the passage of the Holy Will which causes all the distress and uneasiness of life. He has no wish to impose distress and suffering upon us. His Will towards us is pure joy, pure love, pure peace, pure sweetness. This bond of earthly marriage is of the flesh and can be kept by the body, and yet the heart, mind, and soul remain in lovely perfect chastity; and I found that this exquisite freedom – after prolonged endeavours on the part of the soul and the creature – was at length given them as a gift by act of grace, and remained in permanence without variation.

.   .   .

We know that these things are deep mysteries and largely hidden; but this I know: as the heart feels love in itself for God, in that same instant comes God into the soul of the lover. Now, where God is we know that there is neither evil, nor sadness, nor unhappiness, nor any recollection of such things; therefore, to be a great and constant lover to Him is to be automatically lifted from all unhappinesses.

This is our wisest and our best desire, to be a splendid lover to our Most Glorious God.

The more I see of and talk with other people, the more I see how greatly changed I am. I am *freed*. They are bound. I find them bound by fears, by anxieties, by worries, by apprehensions of evil things, by sadness, by fears of death for their loved ones or for themselves. Now, we are freed of all these things *if we keep to the Way*, which is the Road of Love. This change we do not bring about for ourselves, and do not perhaps even realise that it can be effected. For myself, I seemed to be lifted into it, or into a *capacity* for it, on that day and in that moment in which I first loved God. This is not to say that since that moment I have not had to struggle, suffer, and endure, to keep myself in, and progress in this condition; but my sufferings, struggles, and endurances, being for love and in love and because of love, were and are in themselves beautiful, and leave in the recollection nothing inharmonious. They are the difficult prelude to a glorious melody.

Another thing – we become by this love for Him so large that we seem to embrace within our own self the Universe! In some mysterious manner we become in sympathy with all things in the bond of His making.

Are these things worth nothing whatever, that the majority of people should be content to spend their lives looking for five-pound notes and even shillings – and this not only the poor, but the rich more so? I am far more at a loss to understand my fellow-men than I am to understand God. We have need of the shillings, but of other and more lovely things besides, which cost no money and may be had by the poorest. It is rapidly becoming the only sorrow of my life that people do not all come to share this Life in which I live. How that parable knocks at the heart, 'Go out into the high-ways and the hedges and compel them to come in!' To know all this *fullness* of life and not to be able to bring even my nearest and dearest into it: what a terrible mystery is this! – it is an agony. Now, in this agony I share the Agony of Jesus. This is a part of the Cross, and only the Father can make it straight. I see Heaven held out, and *refused*; love held out, and *refused*; perfection shown, and killed upon a cross. What is the crucifix but that most awful of all things – the Grief of God made Visible? Perfect Love submitting itself to the vile freewill of man and dying of wounds! My God! my God! and did *I* ever have a hand in such a thing? I did.

.   .   .

What is it that seems more than any other thing whatever to throw us at last into the arms of God? Suffering. And this not because it is His will (for how much rather would He have us turn to Him in our joy and prosperity), but rather that it is *our* will, that in our earthly joys and prosperities we turn away from Him, and only seek His consolations when we see the failure of our health or happiness. And having by His mercy and forgiveness found Him, we too often and too easily think to glorify ourselves and name each other saints! Did Jesus call us saints? These glorifications mankind would appear to bestow upon itself. He spoke of His flock, and of those who through Him should have life eternal, and of those who, because of the road they take, have their joys in this world only.

.   .   .

When I was being taught to pray for national things and for other persons, and found these prayers answered, I was inclined to be afraid; thinking, What am I that I should dare to petition the Most High? But He showed it me so, which, as in everything, is for all of us: 'It is but a cloud which reflects the glories of the promise of My rainbow; so can the dust, such as thyself, reflect yet other fashions of My will and glory. There is no presumption in the cloud that it should glow with My power; neither is there presumption in thy dust that it should be My vehicle. Both the cloud and thy dust are Mine.'

.   .   .

As we progress in this new way of living we find an increasing difficulty in maintaining petition; for on commencing to petition we will almost invariably be instantly lifted up to such a state of adoration that the whole soul is nothing but a burning song, a thing of living worship. At first I was inclined to blame myself, but now I know that it is acceptable for us to pass from petitioning (no matter who or what for) to high adoration, even though it is a great personal indulgence (and the petitioning is a *hard task*) – an indulgence so extreme that I cannot call to my mind anything in any experience or time of my life, excepting actual raptures, which could, or can, in any way compare or be named in the same breath with this most marvellous joy; for out of this joy of adoration flows the Song of the Soul.

And all these previous years of my life I have lived with the greater part of me dead, and most persons the same! The more I think of it, the more amazed I am at our folly – working and fretting, and striving and looking for every kind of thing except the one thing, beautiful, needful, and living, which is the finding of the personal connection between ourselves and God and the Waters of Life.

Looking to my own experiences, I see clearly how I never could have found without the most powerful and incessant assistance. We are, then, never alone. But first we must have *the will to seek these waters*. This is the secret of the whole matter. He can turn the vilest into a pure lover – if the vilest be willing to have the miracle performed on him! This is the grace of God, and what does it cost Him to pour out this mighty power through us? For everything has its price. My Lord! my Lord! we are not worthy of it all.

This I notice, that when He removes this grace, very shortly the mind goes back to a false, uneven, inharmonious state; so we become like an instrument all out of tune, and are caused indescribable sufferings, like a musician whose ears and nerves are tortured by false notes, while his unmusical neighbours feel no pain! The musician pays a price for the privilege of his great gift; so the lover of Christ.

Again, there is a price to pay for the immeasurable *joy* of prayer, for prayers are not always sweet nor life-giving. The prayers to Christ are always a refreshment, but prayers to the Father may suddenly be turned without any previous thought or private intention into a most awful grief for the abominations of the whole world of us, a terrible wordless burnt-sacrifice of the soul, of unspeakable anguish. And high petitioning is a fearful and profound strain upon the soul and the whole creature.

·   ·   ·

We say that we have need of the purification and conversion of the soul; but rather it is first the conversion of the heart, mind, and will that we have need of. For this would feel to be the drama of our life – the human heart, intelligence, and will are the ego of the creature. Our soul is the visitor within this creature, containing within herself a pure, holy, and incorruptible sparkle of the Divine, and lies choked and atrophied in her human house until revived and awakened by her holy lover; and this awakening is not given to her till the heart and mind of her human house (or the will and spirit of the creature) is in a state of regeneration, or condition to go forward towards God. Which is to say, the creature has been touched by repentance and a desire for the pure and the holy. For if the soul should be awakened to an unrepentant creature, this Will and imperishable worm of the creature (which is of greater coarseness and lustiness than the delicate and fragile soul) will overcome the soul; and this is not the goal, neither is the death of the creature the goal, but the lifting up of the creature into the Divine – this is the goal.

After being awakened, then, in her human house, the soul finds herself locked in with two most treacherous and soiled companions – the human heart and mind; and so great is her loathing and her distress, that for shame's sake these two are constrained to improve themselves. But their progress is slow, and now comes a long and painful time of alternation between two states. At one time the soul will conquer the creature, imposing upon it a sovereign beauty of holiness; and at another the creature will conquer the soul, imposing upon her its hideous designs and desires and causing her many sicknesses. Hence we have the warring which we feel within ourselves, for the soul now desires her home and the creature its appetites.

Until this awakening of the soul takes place, we mistake in thinking that we either live with our soul, or know our soul, or feel with our soul. She does but stir within us from time to time, awaking strange echoes that we do not comprehend; and we live with the mind and the heart and the body only – which is to say, we live as the creature; and this is why on the complete awakening of the soul we feel in the creature an immense and altogether indescribable enhancement of life and of all our faculties, so that in great amazement we say, 'I have never *lived* until this day.' When first the will of the creature is wholly submitted to the lovely guidance of the divine part of the soul, then first we know the ineffable joys of the world of free spirit. For to live with the mind and the body is to be in a state of existence in nature. But to live with the soul is to live above nature, in the immeasurable freedom and intensity of the spirit. And this is the tremendous task of the soul – that she help to redeem the heart and mind from their vileness of the creature and so lift the human upwards with herself to the Divine from whence she came. This, then, is the transmutation or evolution by divine means of the human into the divine; and for this we need to seek repentance or change of heart and mind, which is the will of the creature turning itself towards the beauties of the spirit, that Christ may awaken in us the glories of that sleeping soul which is His bride.

When the soul is fully revived we can know it by this, that we are not able any longer to content ourselves with anything nor anyone save God. Neither are we able to love any save God, for all human desires and loves mysteriously ascend and are merged into the Divine. So, though we love our friend, we love him in God, and in every man perceive but another lover for the Beloved.

.   .   .

To love God might commence to be expressed as being a great quiet, an intense activity, a prodigious joy, and the poignant knowledge of *the immensity of an amazing new life shared.*

The contemplation of God might be expressed as the folding up or complete forgetfulness of all earthly and bodily things, desires, and attractions, and the raising of the heart and mind and the centring of them in great and joyful intensity upon God, by means of love. Of this contemplation of God I find two principal forms: the passive and the active. In the first we are in a state of steady, quiet, and loving perception and reception, and at some farness; in this we are able to remain for hours, entering this state when waking at dawn and remaining in it till rising.

In active contemplation we are in rapturous and

passionate adoration with great nearness, and are not able to remain in it long because of bodily weakness. The soul feels to be never tired by the longest flight, but must return because of the exhaustion of the forlorn and wretched creature, which creature is complete in itself, having its body, of which, being able to touch it, we say, 'It is my body,' and its heart and mind with intelligence, of which we are wont to think, 'This is myself'; yet it is but a part, for the intelligence of our creature is by no means the intelligence of the divine soul, but a far lesser light: for with the intelligence of the divine soul we reach out to God and attain Him, but with the intelligence of the creature we reach towards Him but do not attain, for with it we are unable to penetrate the veil. Therefore, who would know the joys of contemplation must come to them by love, for love is the only means by which the creature can attain. The soul attains God as her birthright, but the creature by adoption and redemption, and this through love. By love the creature dies and is reborn into the spirit.

·   ·   ·

The word 'poverty,' as used to express a necessary condition of our coming to God, is a most misleading term. For how can any condition be rightly named poverty which brings us into the riches of God? Rather let us use the words 'singleness of heart,' or 'simplicity': which is to say, we *put out* all other interests save those pleasing to God (to commence with), and afterwards we reach the condition in which we *have no* interests but in God Himself – the heart and mind and will of the creature becoming wholly God's, and God filling them. How can we say, then, that it is poverty to be filled with God! Rather is it rightly expressed as being a heart fixed in singleness upon God, through drastic simplification of interests: the which is no poverty, but the wealth of all the Universe.

.   .   .

Some of us seem open to suggestion, others to the steadier effects of personal influence. I never came under the personal influence of another except once, when I came under the influence of the being I loved most – my brother. At ten he saved my life from drowning, and at eighteen his influence and total lack of faith in God, coupled with the searchings and probings of my own intelligence, took me away from God, in whom I had previously had a comfortable faith. At seventeen I began to lap up the hardest scientific books as a cat laps milk. I said to myself, 'I must find truth, I must find out what everything really is'; but I could not reconcile science with Church teaching. I was not able to adjust the truths of science – which were demonstrable to both senses and intelligence – with the unprovable dogmas set forth by the Church as necessary to salvation.

I slowly and surely lost what faith I had, and hung a withered heart upon the pitiless and nameless bosom of the Cosmos. Inward life became for me a horrible emptiness without hope. Surrounded with gaieties and the innumerable social successes of youth, I found that neither science nor society could satisfy my soul, or that something living within me which knew a terrible necessity for God. For two long and dreadful years I fought secretly and desperately to regain this lost belief, and when at last I succeeded there remained a monstrous and impenetrable wall between myself and God. But by comparison with the horrors of past loneliness it was heaven to me to feel Him there, even behind that wall. (Now that I have found Him by love, I am able to return to science as to a most exquisite unrolling of the majesty of His truths and powers and laws, and am brought nearer and nearer to Him the more I learn of science.) Outside the wall I remained for more than twenty years, seeking and searching for an opening in that mighty barrier.

And after more than twenty years I found the Door – and it was Jesus Christ.

. . .

Lately I have seen the word 'contemplation' used as expressing the heights of attainment in God-consciousness of men, and I find it inadequate. From the age of seventeen I fell into the habit of contemplation, not of God, but of Nature:

which is to say, I would first place myself, sitting, in such a position that my body would not fall and I might completely forget it, and then would look about me and drink in the beauty of the scene, my eyes coming finally to rest upon the spot most beautiful to me. There they remained fixed. All thoughts were now folded up so that my mind, flowing singly in one direction, concentrated itself upon the beauty on which I gazed. This soon vanished, and I saw nothing whatever, but, bearing away into a place of complete silence and emptiness, I there assimilated and enjoyed inwardly the soaring essence of the beauty which I had previously drawn into my mind through my eyes, being now no longer conscious of seeing outwardly, but living entirely from the inward. This I did almost every day, but to do it I was obliged to seek solitude, and absolute solitude is a hard thing to find; but I sought it, no matter where, even in a churchyard! I saw no graves. I saw the sky, or a marvellous cloud pink with the kisses of the sun, and away I went. I judge this now to have been contemplation, though I never thought of it by so fine-sounding a name; it was only my delightful pastime, yet there was a strange inexpressible sadness in it. Nature and beauty were not enough. The more beauty I saw, the more I longed for something to which I could not put a name. At times the ache of this pain became terrible, almost agonising, but I could not forgo my pastime. Now, at last, I know what this pain was: my soul looked for God, but my creature did not know it. For just in this same way we contemplate God, savouring Him without seeing Him, and being filled to the brim with marvellous delights with no sadness.

But this condition of contemplation is very far from being the mountain-top; it is but a high plateau from which we make the final ascent. The summit is an indescribable contact, and this summit is not one summit but many summits. Which is to say, we have contact of several separate forms – that of giving, that of receiving, and that of immersion or absorption, which *at its highest* is altogether unendurable as fire.

Of this last I am able only to say this: that not only is it inexpressible by any words, but that that which is a state of extreme beatitude to the soul is death to the creature by excess of joy. Therefore both heart and mind fear to recall any details of the memory of this highest attainment. I knew it but once. To know it again would be the death of my body. For more than two hours (as well as I am able to judge) before becoming to this highest experience, my soul travelled through what felt to be an ocean, for she rose and fell upon billows in a state of infinite bliss.

Of other forms of contact we have a swift, unexpected, even unsought for attainment, which is entirely of His volition; that sudden condescension to the soul, in which in unspeakable rapture she is caught up to her holy lover.

These are the topmost heights which the creature dare recall, though to the soul they remain in memory as life itself. The variations of these forms of contact are infinite, for God would seem to will to be both eternal changelessness and variation in infinitude.

Because of this, and the marvellous depths and heights and breadths of life revealed to her, the soul is able to conceive of an eternity of bliss, for monotony ceases to be joy. In Nature we see that no two trees in a forest are alike, and two fruits gathered from one bough have not the same flavour.

But to my feeling all degrees of attainment are only to be distinguished as varying degrees of union, the joy of which is of a form and a degree of intensity and purity which can enter neither the heart nor the mind to imagine, but must be experienced to be understood, and when experienced remains in part incomprehensible. It is not to be obtained by force of the will, neither can it be obtained without the will. It is, then, a mystery of two wills in unison, in which our will is temporarily fused into and consumed by the will of God and is in transports of felicity over its own annihilation! This is outside reason and therefore incomprehensible to the creature, but comprehensible to the soul, and becomes the aim and object of our life to attain in permanence, and is the uttermost limit of all conceivable rapture.

When I first knew union and contact upon the

hill I had the impression of a very great light outside of me. I never again had an outward impression of it.

But when any sense of inward *light* is felt I consider it to be a high ecstasy and hard for the body. It is the sweet and gentle touchings of Christ which are the great and unspeakable comfort of both soul and body. Inward heat I never felt till many months after my third conversion and more than four years from my first conversion. This extraordinary sensation, which to my mind is like a magnetic seething with heat and ravishment of joy, I felt inwardly only after I had learnt to know a sudden, secret, joyous delight of love in the soul, which is easiest described as sweetness of love, is from the Christ, and *very frequently* given by Him. And some six months after the heat, fire, electric seething, or however best it may be named, I first knew the song of the soul. Now, although it is better not to dwell upon the memory of past spiritual joys, lest we become greedy, and equally wise not to dwell upon the memory of anguishes, lest we fall into self-pity, which of all emotions is the most sickly and useless (and our wisest is to live only from hour to hour with all the sweetness that we can, leaving to Him the choosing of our daily bread, whether it be high joy or pain), still I confess that I have thought over and compared these joys sufficiently to know very well which I love the best. Heat of love is very wonderful, and sweetness is very lovely, and raptures and ecstasies are outside words; but most beautiful of all is the song of the soul, and this is when – in highest adoration – passing beyond heat, and further than sweetness, the soul goes up alone upon the highest summit of love, and there like a bird pours out the rapturous and golden passion of her love. And His Spirit, biding very near, never touches her; for if He touch, it is at once an ecstasy, and because of the stress of this she would have neither words nor song with which to rejoice Him.

Oh, the pure happiness of the soul in this wonderful song!

Truly I think it is greater than in the rapture or the ecstasy, because in these the soul receives, but in the song, mounting right up to Him, she gives. And now at last we know the fuller meaning of Christ's words where He says: 'It is more blessed to give than to receive.'

Beloved, Thou takest the creature and liftest it up; Thou takest the creature and liftest it high, so that nevermore can it offend Thee, and the soul is free to sing of her love. Then is it Thy will that the creature should love Thee? Or is it Thy will that the soul should adore? Beloved, I know not whether with my heart and mind I most adore Thee, or whether with my soul I love Thee more. And where is that secret trysting-place of love? I do not know; for whilst I go there and whilst I return I am blind, and whilst I am there I am blinded by Love Himself.

O wondrous trysting-place! which is indeed the only trysting-place of all the world worthy to be named.

For every other love on earth is but a poor, pale counterfeit of love – a wan Ophelia, wandering with a garland of sad perished flowers to crown the dust.

.　　.　　.

As the loving creature progresses he will find himself ceasing to live in things, or thoughts of things or of persons, but his whole mind and heart will be concentrated upon the thought of God alone. Now Jesus, now the High Christ, now the Father, but never away from one of the aspects or personalities of God, though his conditions of nearness will vary. For at times he will be in a condition of great nearness, at times in a condition of some farness, or, more properly speaking, of obscurity. He will be in a condition of waiting (this exceedingly frequent, the most frequent of all); a condition of amazing happiness; a condition of pain, of desolation at being still upon the earth instead of with God. He will be in a condition of giving love to God, or a condition of receiving love, of remembrance and attention. He will be in a condition of immeasurable glamour, an extraordinary illumination of every faculty, not by any act of his own, but poured through him until he is filled with the elixir of some new form of life, and feels himself before these experiences never to have lived – he but existed as a part of Nature. But now, although he is become more united to Nature than ever before, he also is mysteriously drawn apart from her, without being in any way presumptuous, he feels to be above her, not by any merits but by intention of Another. He is become lifted up into the spirit and essence of Nature, and the heavy and more obvious parts of her bind him no more. He is in a condition of freedom, he is frequently in a condition of great splendour, and is wrapped perpetually round about with that most glorious mantle – God-consciousness.

These are man's right and proper conditions. These are the lovely will of God for us. And too many of us have the will to go contrary to Him. Oh, the tragedy of it! If the whole world of men and women could be gathered and lifted into this garden of love! Persuaded to rise from lesser loves into the bosom of His mighty Love!

For the truly loving soul here on earth there are no longer heavens, nor conditions of heavens, nor grades, nor crowns, nor angels, nor archangels, nor saints, nor holy spirits; but, going out and up and on, we reach at last THE ONE, and for marvellous unspeakably glorious moments KNOW HIM.

This is life: to be in Him and He in us, *and know it*.

.   .   .

These beautiful flights of the soul cannot be

taken through idleness, though they are taken in what would outwardly appear to be a great stillness. This stillness is but the necessary abstraction from physical activity, even from physical consciousness; but inwardly the spirit is in a great activity, a very ferment of secret work. This, to the writer, is frequently produced by the beautiful in Nature, the spirit involuntarily passing at the sight of beauty into a passionate admiration for the Maker of it. This high, pure emotion, which is also an *intense activity* of the spirit, would seem so to etherealise the creature that instantly the delicate soul is able to escape her loosened bonds and flies towards her home, filled with ineffable, incomparable delight, praising, singing, and joying in her Lord and God until the body can endure no more, and swiftly she must return to bondage in it. But the most wonderful flights of the soul are made during a high adoring contemplation of God. We are in high contemplation when the heart, mind, and soul, having dropped consciousness of all earthly matters, have been brought to a full concentration upon God – God totally invisible, totally unimaged, *and yet focussed to a centre-point by the great power of love*. The soul, whilst she is able to maintain this most difficult height of contemplation, may be visited by an intensely vivid perception, inward vision, and knowledge of God's attributes or perfections, very brief; and this *as a gift*, for she is not able to will such a felicity to herself, but being given such she is instantly consumed with adoration, and *enters ecstasy.*

Having achieved these degrees of progress, the heart and mind will say: 'Now I may surely repose for I have attained!' And so we may repose, but not in idleness, which is to say, not without abundance of prayer. For only by prayer is our condition maintained and renewed; but without prayer, by which I mean an incessant inward communion, quickly our condition changes and wears away. No matter to what degree of love we have attained we need to pray for more; without persistent but short prayer for faith and love we might fall back into strange woeful periods of cold obscurity.

To the accomplished lover great and wonderful is prayer; the more completely the mind and heart are lifted up in it, the slower the wording. The greater the prayer, the shorter in words, though the longer the saying of it, for each syllable will needs be held up upon the soul before God, slowly and, as it were, in a casket of fire, and with marvellous joy. And there are prayers without words, and others without even thoughts, in which the soul in a great stillness passes up like an incense to the Most High. This is very pure, great love; wonderful, high bliss.

.   .   .

In the earlier stages of progress, when the heart and mind suffer from frequent inconstancy, loss of warmth, even total losses of love, set the heart and mind to recall to themselves by reading or thinking some favourite aspect of their Lord Jesus Christ. It may be His gentleness, or His marvellous forgiveness, as to Peter when 'He turned and looked at him' after the denial; for so He turns and looks upon ourselves. Or it may be His sweetness that most draws us. But let us fasten the heart and mind upon whichever it may be, and in the warmth of admiration *love will return to us.*

．　　　．　　　．

The mode of entrance into active contemplation I would try to convey in this way. The body must be placed either sitting or kneeling, and supported, or flat on the back as though dead. Now the mind must commence to fold itself, closing forwards as an open rose might close her petals to a bud again, for every thought and image must be laid away and nothing left but a great forward-moving love intention. Out glides the mind all smooth and swift, and plunges deep, then takes an upward curve and up and on till willingly it faints, the creature dies, and consciousness is taken over by the soul, which, quickly coming to the trysting-place, *spreads herself* and there awaits the revelations of her God. To my feeling this final complete passing over of consciousness from the mind to the soul is by act and will of God only, and cannot be performed by will of the creature, and is the fundamental difference between the contemplation of

Nature and the contemplation of God. The creature worships, but the soul alone knows contact. And yet the mode of contemplation is a far simpler thing than all these words – it is the very essence of simplicity itself; and in this sublime adventure we are really conscious of no mode nor plan nor flight, nought but the mighty need of spirit to Spirit and love to Love.

.   .   .

The picking out and choosing of certain persons, and the naming of them 'elect' and 'chosen' souls, when I first read of it, filled me with such a sinking that I tried, when coming upon the words, not to admit the meaning of them into myself; for that some should be chosen and some not I felt to be favouritism, and could not understand or see the justice of it. I never ask questions. He left me in this condition for eighteen months. Then He led me to an explanation sufficient for me. The way He showed it me was not by comparisons with great things – angels and saints and holy persons; but by that humble creature, man's friend, the dog, He showed me the elect creature. It was this way.

One evening as I passed through the city I had one of those sudden strong impulses (by which He guides us) to go to a certain and particular cinematograph exhibition. I was very tired, and tried to put away the thought, but it pressed in the way that I know, and I knew it better to go. I sat for an hour seeing things that had no interest for me, and wondering why I should have had to come, when at last a film was shown of war-dogs in training – dogs trained especially to assist men and to carry their messages.

These dogs were especially selected, not for their charm of outward appearance, but for their inward capacities; *not for an especial love of the dog* (or favouritism), but for that which they were willing to learn how to do. The qualifications for (s)election were willingness, obedience, fidelity, endurance. Once chosen they were set apart. Then commenced the training, and we were shown how man put his will through the dog: he was able to do this *only because of the willingness of the dog.* The purport of the training was to carry a message for his master wherever his master willed. He must go instantly and at full speed; he must leap any obstacle; he must turn away from his own kind if they should entice him to linger on the way; he must subdue all his natural desires and instincts entirely to his master's desires; he must be indifferent to danger. And to secure this he was fired over by numbers of men, difficulties were set for him, and he was distracted from his straight course by a number of tests. Yet we saw the brave and faithful creatures running on their way at their fullest speed until, exhausted and breathless but filled with joy of *love and willingness*, they reached the journey's end, to be caressed and cared for beyond other dogs until the next occasion should arise. Then we were shown the dog in his fully-trained condition. His master could now always rely upon him. A dog always ready, always faithful and self-forgetful, was then set apart into a still smaller and more (s)elect group and surrounded with most especial care and love. Never would it want for anything. In this there was justice. Forsaking all their natural ways, these dogs had submitted themselves wholly, in loving willingness, to their master's will, and he in return would lavish all his best on them. It was but just. Oh, how my heart leaped over it! At last I understood – for as the dog, so the human creature. We become chosen souls, not for our own sakes (which had always seemed to me such favouritism), but for our willingness to learn our Master's will. And what is His will and what is His work? Of many, many kinds, and this is shown to the soul in her training. But the hardest to learn is not that of the worker, but of the messenger and lover. As the messenger, to take His messages, in whatever direction, instantly and correctly, and to take back the answer from man to Himself – which is to say, to hold before Him the needs of man on the fire of the soul, known to most persons under the name of prayer. And as the lover, to sing to Him with never-failing joyful love and thanks.

But the learning and work of the soul is not so simple as that of the dog, who carries the message in writing upon his collar. The soul can have no written paper to assist her, and long and painful is her training; and exquisitely sweet it is when, having swiftly and accurately taken the message, she waits before Him for the rapture of those caresses that she knows so well.

How I was spurred! For I said, 'Shall dogs outdo us in love and devotion?' Only in a condition of total submission, self-forgetfulness, self-abnegation, can the soul either receive or deliver her message. In this way she is justified of the joys of her election. The dog, faithful in all ways to his master, receives in return all praise and all meats, whatever he desires. The faithful soul also receives all praise and all meats, both spiritual and carnal, for nothing of earthly needs will lack her *if she asks*; and without asking, her needs are mysteriously and completely given her. Her spiritual meats are, in this world, peace, joy, ecstasy, rapture; and of the world to come it is written that eye hath not seen, nor ear heard, neither have entered into the heart of man, the things that God has prepared for them that love Him.

It might be supposed that only persons filled with public charities and social improvements, ardent and painstaking church workers, might most surely and easily learn to be messengers. But all these persons pursue and follow their own line of thought, the promptings of their own minds and hearts. They are admirable workers, but not messengers. For the hound of God must have in his heart no plan of his own. It is hard for the heart to say, 'I have no wishes of my own; I have no interests, no plans, no ambitions, no schemes, no desires, no loves, no will. Thy will is my will. Thy desire is my desire. Thy love is my all. I am empty of all things, that I may be a channel for the stream of Thy will.'

With what patience, what tenderness, what inexpressible endearments He helps the soul, training her by love! – which is not to say that she is trained without much suffering of the creature. So we are trained by two opposite ways – by suffering and by joys; and the whole under an attitude of passionate and devoted attention on our part. The sufferings of the soul baffle all description with their strange intensities.

Our encouragements are great and extraordinary sweetnesses, urgings, and joyful uplifting of the spirit. So that when we would stop, we are pressed forward; when we are exhausted, we are filled with the wine of sweetness; when we are in tears, we are embraced into the Holy Spirit.

.   .   .

Sin and ill are the false notes struck by man across the harmony of God's will, and to strike upon or even remember such notes is instant banishment from the music of His presence. Where all is joy, there joy is all; and he who has not reached this joy does not know God – he is still a follower, and not a possessor, and he should refuse in his heart to remain satisfied with his condition, but climb on. Why stay behind? Climb on, climb on!

How often I have been mystified and disturbed by the attitude of many religious and pious people, that to follow Christ is a way of gloom, of sadness, of heaviness! How often have I gathered from sermons that we are to give up all bright and enticing things if we would follow Him, and the preacher *goes no further*! Has the Lord, then, no enticements, no sweetnesses, no brightness to offer us, that we should be asked to forsake all pleasantnesses, all brightness, all attractions, if we follow Him? This to me always seemed terrible and my heart would sink. Indeed, to my poor mind and heart it seemed nothing more hopeful than a going from bad to worse!

All the pictures I have seen, either of the Crucifixion or the Way of the Cross (and especially those of more recent times and painting), portray His Blessed Face all worn with gloom; and I know now that this is far from the truth. For perfect love knows agony, but no gloom. He went through all His agony, lifted high above gloom, in a great ecstasy of love for us.

To speak of *sacrifice* in connection with following Him, is to my mind, the work of a very foolish person and one in danger of being blasphemous. For how dare we say that it is a sacrifice when, by the putting away of foolish desires, we find God! And to find God, through the following of

Jesus Christ, is to *gain so much* (even in this world, and without waiting for the next) that those who gain it never cease to be amazed at the vastness of it.

We find this to be an absolute truth, that if we have not Him we have, and are, nothing, in comparison with that which we are and that which we have when we have Him.

In my earlier stages I was greatly set back and disturbed by this gloom and sacrifice (which is no sacrifice) of myself so put forward by pulpit teaching. It was a great hindrance to me and blinded me to the truth. I was only a normal, ordinary creature, and they thrust a great burden into my arms.

Little by little, as I was able to learn directly from His own heart, I came to know Him as He is; and I could not reconcile this knowledge of Himself which He gave me, especially of His high willingness and serenity, with pulpit teachings of heavy gloom. The Church too frequently spoke to me of following Him in terms which conveyed a burden: 'Pick up thy cross, pick up thy cross!' they cried; and He spoke to me in terms which conveyed a great joy: 'Come to Me, come to Me, for I love thee!'

I thought I was very cowardly and sinned by this inability to like the gloomy burden, and one day I came upon this out of Jeremiah: 'As for the prophet, or the priest, or the people, that shall say, The burden of the Lord, I will punish that man and his house . . . because ye say, The burden of the Lord, I will utterly forget you and forsake you, and cast you out of My presence.'

These words of Jesus, 'Take up thy cross and follow Me': whoever will do it will be shown by Jesus that the cross of following Him is no burden, but a deliverance, a finding of life, the way of escape, a great joy, and a garland of love.

The world thinks of joyousness as being laughter, cackling, and much silly noise; and to such I do not speak. But the Christ's joyousness is of a high, still, marvellous, and ineffable completeness – beyond all words; and *wholly satisfying* to heart and soul and body and mind.

It is written, 'They shall love silver, and not be satisfied with it' – for why? Only those are *satisfied* who know the gold of Christ.

All of which is not to say that by following Him we shall escape from happenings and inconveniences and sorrows and illnesses common to life; but that when these come we are raised out of our distress into His ineffable peace.

When the heart is sad, use this sadness in a comprehension of the deeper pain of Jesus, who was in the selfsame exile as we ourselves. The more the soul is truly awakened and touched, the more she feels herself to be in exile; and this is her cross.

But the remedy for her sadness is that she should courageously pass out of her woes of exile and go up to meet her lover with smiles. Now,

He cannot resist this smiling courage and love of the soul, and very quickly He must send her His sweetness, and her sadness is gone.

.   .   .

When I say that if we will take a few steps alone towards Christ – which is to say, if we will make some strenuous efforts to cleanse ourselves and change our minds and ways – He will take us all the rest of the way, I speak from experience. For amongst many things this happened to me: at a certain stage, after my third conversion on the hill, He caused my former thoughts, desires, and follies to go away from me! It was as though He had sent a veil between me and such thoughts of my heart and mind as might not be pleasing to Him, so that they disappeared from my knowledge and my actions!

By this marvellous act He removed my difficulties, and put me into a state of innocence which resembled the innocence I remember to have had up to the age of four or five years. But I find this new innocence far more wonderful than that of childhood, which is but the innocence of ignorance. But this new innocence – which is a gift of God – is innocence with knowledge. I am not able to express the gratitude and amazement and wonder that have never ceased to fill me about this. Such things can only be spoken of by the soul to her lover, and then not in words but in a silence of tears.

What did I ever do that He should show me such kindness? I did nothing except this: I desired with all the force of my heart and soul and mind and body to love Him. I said, 'Oh, if I could be the warmest, tenderest lover that ever Thou didst have! Teach me to be Thy burning lover.' This was my perpetual prayer. And my idea of Heaven was and is this, that without so much as knowing, or being known or perceived by *any save Himself*, without even a name, yet retaining my full consciousness of individuality, I should be with Him for always.

What is this love for God, and how define it? For myself, I never knew it until I was filled with it upon the hill. Many judge it to be a *following* of Christ and His wishes, but this is only a part of it and the way we begin it, and often we begin from duty, fear of future punishment, desire for salvation or spiritual pre-eminence, and obedience; and in none of these is there the joy of love.

By such standards I might count myself to have loved Him for twenty years; but know I did not. For ten years past I felt myself to have so great a need of Him, I sought Him so, that for me Heaven contained no re-met former earthly loves, much as I loved them here. I knew that He would be my all. Nevertheless, He was not yet my Love, but my Need.

Love is a fire, for we feel the great heat of it.

Love is a light, for we perceive the white glare of it.

Of things known, to what can we compare it? Most perhaps to electricity, for here we have both light and heat, and the lightning flash strikes that which already contains the most of itself (or electricity). And the lightning of God's love strikes him whose heart contains the most love for Himself. And He strikes when He will and afterwards visits when He will; and I do not count myself (for all my earthly loves) to have so much as known the outer edge of the meaning of the word love, till He struck me with His own upon that hill.

Truly, fair and holy love is our warranty, our only pass for entering into Heaven.

Brave and wilful, rapturous and insistent, love passes with bold yet humble ecstasy into the very presence of her Lord and God; and alone, out of all creation, is never denied the Right of Way.

.   .   .

I have seen it quoted, 'Turn to the heights, turn to the deeps, turn within, turn without, everywhere thou shalt find the Cross.' But I see it so: 'Turn to the heights, turn to the deeps, turn within, turn without, everywhere thou shalt find His Love.' Love to help on the way. Too much we might suppose, to hear pious people talk, that because of Christ's way we must be miserable and our life an endless Cross! And so life may be a cross, but He carries it for us.

Do sinful men never suffer? Do the sinful

escape disease? – and live for ever without biting the dust in death or disappointment? Why, disease and suffering are the very twin-children of sin. I am amazed that people can take such a view of the Cross as to think it an unhappy, miserable way. For so marvellous is the beauty of such love that there is no other so desirable a thing upon earth.

'Come, walk the way with Me,' says the Beloved; 'I am all serenity, all peace, all might, all power, all love. Come, walk with Me, and forget thy tiny cares in the peace of My bosom.'

.   .   .

We do not love God because we do not yet know Him. And we do not know Him because we seek only to know and have our own desires: and having learnt to know these, we would have our unknown God accommodate Himself to us and them.

But let us first seek to know God's desires by heart, and then accommodate our own to His: so shall we learn to be pleasing to Christ, that He may lead us, whilst here, into His Garden. For to the creature that ardently pursues God there comes at last a time when He reveals Himself to the searching soul, saying: 'I Am Here. Come!' Then in secrecy we arise, – and go to Him out of the House of Vanity into the music of the great Beyond.

There is small credit or virtue to the soul when,

in a state of high grace or nearness, she burns with love for her God: for she is under the spell of the enticement of His Presence – how can she help but burn! It is as though two earthly lovers, in full sight and nearness, are filled each for each with great love, and are content.

But this is a credit to the soul and the creature (as to the earthly lovers), that in separation and farness they should seek no other, but continue to dwell with great intentness upon the absent love. This is fidelity.

At times it is as if her Lord said to the soul: 'I have other to do than to stay by thee; and also thou hast had more than enough to thy share of My honey'; and, so saying, He departs.

And this is fidelity of the soul and the creature, and a great virtue, that, without change of face, without complaint or petitioning, they should with all sweetness continue to pour up to Him their unabated love. If any can do this, he is a perfect lover and has no more to learn.

When the love of the soul, as it were, exceeds itself, it passes up and beyond even the song of love; and being unable to express itself by words or by song, or by deep sighings, or by any of those subtle, silent, spiritual means known only between herself and God, when all means fail because of the too great stress of her adoration, then the soul passes into a great pain, which is the anguish of love and a hard thing to bear. This excess is to the fullness of the Godhead.

And now the soul must turn to prayer for help, but not to the Godhead: for the more she turns to the Godhead the greater becomes her anguish. But coming down to His humanity, she must beseech sweet Jesus for His aid, and so regain her equilibrium.

.   .   .

Many of us are, perhaps unwittingly, impudent to God. In this way we are impudent: We question (even though it be in secret, hidden in the heart and not spoken) the justice of God, the ways of God, the plans of God, the love of God: by which means we argue with God and judge Him. And another manner of impudence we have is this, that we dare to attribute or to blame Him for the results of man's own filth, saying: 'This and this is the will of God, for we see that it exists, and His will is omnipotent.' Oh, beware of this impudence, drop it out of the heart and mind, and flee from it as from the plague! 'How then can these things be, if He is omnipotent?' we say. Because of this, that in the trust of His great love He gave us the royal and Godly gift of freewill, and our souls have proved themselves unworthy to have it; and now the creature is brought before the Beautiful, and the Holy, and the Pure, but turning away, like the sow, prefers the mire and the festering sores proceeding from such wallowings. If there were no choice, there were no virtue, and no progress home. But let no man venture in his heart to attribute to that Holy and Marvellous Being whom we speak of as God, not knowing as yet His Name, any will towards festers and corruptions, for what does He say Himself? 'Their sins rise up before Me and stink in My nostrils!'

We surely forget that this world is not yet God's Kingdom, and that His will is not done here, and will not be until the Judgment Day. This world is but a tiny testing-chamber in His mighty workshop; and great and wonderful is the care He has for the workers in it.

O man! whence come thy wretchednesses? Look round and think. Do they not all proceed from self and fellow-men, alive or dead? Then why blame God?

'Why am I here?' we cry, 'to suffer all these pains, and my consent not asked? A poor, sad puppet dancing to a tune I know not the rhythm of. Where is my recompense? And where my wages? I will take all I can of what is offered here, and give no thanks! It is but my scant due for all my wretchednesses!'

O foolish man! so timid of all future possibilities of bliss that he must grasp and burn himself with such delights as he finds here! And equally mistaken and small-minded man who thinks that all our Mighty God will have to offer us hereafter are crowns, damp clouds and mists, and endless hymns! Such little hearts are far away indeed from knowing the *magnitudes of Life*.

O wretched man! why this distrust? Hast thou created even thine own palate and digestion? Hast thou invented any of those fond delights that so enslave thee now? Hast thou thyself devised the means wherewith to satisfy the longing of thy *creature* for the sweets of life? They were provided thee; all that thou hast created is misuse! Thou art but a perverted thing! – a crooked tool of self, a fly drowning in the honey that it sought too greedily to own!

O wretched, wretched man! so cloyed with sweets of earth thou canst not raise thy head to see the sunrise out beyond the world, and know true sweets! How many are the tears wept over thee by the great heart of God!

. . .

Since coming into this new way of living, the more I come into contact with music the more I sense a mysterious connection between melody – the soul – and her *origin*. Alone out of all the sciences and arts, music has no foundation upon anything on earth. There is no music in nature until the soul, come to a perfect harmony within herself, brings out the hidden harmony in all creation, and, turning it to melody within herself, returns it to her Lord in song, whether by outward instrument or inward love.

The soul, indeed, would seem to have come out of a life of infinite melody and to have dropped into an existence of mere contrary and vexing time-beat.

Who can by any means account for the variety of passions excited within him by the mere difference of the spacing, time, or rhythm of music? In my new condition of living I notice that the soul throws out with most disdainful impatience music that was formerly beautiful to my mind and heart (or my creature); and certain types of flowing cadences (very rarely to be found) sustained in high, flowing, delicate, and soaring continuity will produce in her conditions akin to a madness of joy. For one brief instant *she remembers! but cannot utter what!*

Of visions I know nothing, but received all my experiences into my soul as amazingly real inward perceptions. That these perceptions are of unprecedented intensity, and more realistic than those which are merely visual, can be understood by bodily comparisons; for to *feel* or to be one with fire is more than to *see* it.

To try to compare spiritual life with physical experiences would seem to be useless; for, to my feeling, while we live in the spirit we live at a great speed, – indeed, an incalculably great speed – and as a whole and not in parts. For with physical living we live at one moment by the eyes, at another with the mind, at another through the heart, at another with the body. But the spirit feels to have no parts, for all parts are of so perfect a concordance that in this marvellous harmony all is one and one is all. And this with *incredible intensity*, so that we live not as now – dully – but at white heat of sensibility.

Prayer

Prayer is the golden wedding-ring between ourselves and God. For myself, I divide it into two halves – the one petitioning, the other offering.

Of petitioning I would say that this is the *work* of the soul; and of offering, that it is the pleasure of the soul.

Of petitioning, that I come to it under His command; and of offering, that I come to it of my own high, passionate desire.

I make upon my knees, three times a day, three short and formal prayers of humble worship as befits the creature worshipping its Ineffable and Mighty God: and for the rest of my time I sing to Him from my heart and soul, as befits the joyful lover, adoring and conversing with the Ineffable and Exquisite Beloved.

.   .   .

This is the circle of His way with us. First is prayer; then love; and after love, humility. With humility comes grace; and after grace, temptation; and in temptation we must quickly enter prayer again.

.   .   .

O wonderful and ineffable God! who, while remaining hidden from His lovers in this life, yet so ravishes their hearts and minds and souls that they are unable to find truly sweet even the greatest of life's former joys – for nothing can now ever satisfy them but the secret and marvellous administrations of His love and grace! On one day feeling to be forsaken, the most desolate and lonely of all creatures in the Universe; and on another exalted to almost unbearable pinnacles of bliss, equal to the angels in felicity, and blest beyond all power of words to say – such and so are the lovers of God.

.   .   .

The soul has six wings: love, obedience, humility, simplicity, perseverance, and courage. With these she can attain God.

We know very well that no man will find God either enclosed, held fast, or demonstrated within a circle of dogmatic words; but every man can find, in his own soul, an exquisite and incomparable instrument of communication with God. To establish the working of this communication is the whole object and meaning of life in this world – this world of material, finite, and physical things, in which the human body is at once a means and a debt.

The key to progress is a continual dressing of the will and mind and heart towards God, best brought about by continually filling the heart and mind with beautiful, grateful, and loving thought of Him. At all stages of progress the thoughts persistently fly away to other things in the near and visible world, and we have need quietly and perpetually to pick them up and re-centre them on Him. With the mind turned in this way, steadily towards God, we are in that state known to science as polarisation: we are in that condition in which common iron becomes a magnet. It is so that God transforms us into a diminutive part-likeness of Himself.

When at last the soul reaches union with Him, she is for a while so caressed, so held in a perpetual contact and nearness, that we may think ourselves already permanently entered into Paradise! But this is not the plan; and, our education being exceedingly incomplete, we return to our schooling.

We commence to experience profound and even terrible longings to leave the world and all creatures, for we cannot bear either the sight or the sound of them, and seek all day long to be alone with the Beloved God. To conquer this last selfishness and weakness of the soul we must go again – as in the beginning – to Jesus. He teaches us to go to and fro *willingly*, gladly, from the highest to the lowest. To pick up our daily life and duties, our obligations to a physical world, in all humility, sweet reasonableness, and submission. He teaches us willingly to accept incessant interruptions, and with smiling face and perfect inward smoothness to descend from a high contemplation of God (and only those who know high contemplation can judge of the immensity of what I say) to listen and *attend to* some most trivial want of a fellow-creature! Reader, it is the hardest thing of all. No sooner have we learnt the hard and difficult way of ascent than we must willingly come down it, even remain altogether in the valley below, and that with a smiling face and, if possible, no thought of impatience! This is the true sacrifice of the soul. Now, the sacrifices of the creature are the giving up of the near and visible joys and prides of the world to follow Christ, and are not real but seeming sacrifices, for, if done heartily and with courage, an exchange between these joys and the joys of the invisible is rapidly effected, and there remains no sacrifice, but 'the hidden treasure' is ours! But the sacrifice of the soul is real and long; for having at last re-found God, she must resign her full joy of Him till the death of the body – and this willingly, thankfully, without complaint, not asking favours but pouring up her gratitude. In joy or in pain, in happiness or in tribulation – gratitude! gratitude! – and this not by her own strength but by strength of the Holy Ghost.

.   .   .

Because of this new way of living, the mind acquires a great increase of capacity and strength and clearness: being able to deal quickly and correctly with all matters brought before it with an ease previously altogether unknown to its owner. It is no exaggeration to say that the sagacity, scope, and grasp of the mind feels to be more than doubled from that which it previously was, and this not because of any study, but by an involuntary alteration. So that, though the mind and attention are now given almost exclusively to the things of God, yet when the things of the world have to be dealt with, this is accomplished with extraordinary efficiency and quickness, though very distasteful to the mind.

.　　.　　.

As the soul returns to her source nothing is more strongly emphasised to her than the strength and intensity of individuality; she is shown that the essence of all joy is Individuality in Union.

In the marvellous condition of Contact, though we cease to be the creature or the soul adoring the Creator (but by an incomprehensible condescension we are accepted as one with Himself in love), yet we retain our own consciousness, which is our individuality.

In the highest rapture I ever was in, my soul passed into a fearful extremity of experience: she was burned with so terrible an excess of bliss, that she was in great fear and anguish because of this excess. Indeed, she was so overcome by this too great realisation of the strength of God that she was in terror of both God and joy. It was three days before she recovered any peace, and more than a year before I dared recall one instant of it to mind.

I am not able to think that even in Heaven the soul could endure such heights for more than a period. These heights are incomparably, unutterably beyond vision and union. They are the uttermost extremity of that which can be endured by the soul, at least until she has re-risen to great altitudes of holiness in ages to come.

By contact with God we acquire certain wonderful and terrible realisations of truth and knowledge. For one thing, we learn the nature and mode of spirit-life, as over against body- or sense-life. We learn, at first with great fear, something of the awful intensities of pain, as of joy, which can be endured by the spirit when free of the body: for when we are in the spirit we do not *see* fire, but we feel to *become it* and yet live! And so equally of pain or joy — we do not feel these things delicately, as with, and in, the body, but we pass into the essence of these things themselves, in all their terrible and marvellous intensity, which is comparatively without limit.

Woe to those who must gather the garland of pain — which is remorse — after death! It is easier to suffer a whole lifetime in the body than one day in the spirit. O soul! come to thy contrition here in this world, where pain has short limit! Repent and return!

.   .   .

Of the marvellous favours shown to the soul the heart cries out: 'O mighty God! of the magnitude of Thy condescensions I am afraid even to think; they are too great for me, and I dare to recall them, but only with all the simplicity of a little child!'

.   .   .

Those who feel desire and need within themselves to reach the heights of inward life will do it best, not through diversity of interests in fellow-creatures, but by unification of all interests in God.

God once found, and possessed, we return to the interests of creatures in moderation and with judgment.

.   .   .

What is pain? It is a mystery of separation, and we are gangrenous with sin and pain because of separation from the source of life.

Truth now comes to us in such small segments that we no longer see the pattern of it; but this we are able to perceive: that the mystery of Separation is equal in degree with the mystery of Union, and that the child of separation is Pain.

How did the soul ever become so separated from God? To my feeling, in curiosity of loves we may find the answer, and know the 'fall' to be not that of the animal man but of the soul, which, once living in perpetual beatitude – knowing nothing of pain because of the unity with God, not understanding or being even grateful for her bliss because of its invariable presence, and given free will, – in curiosity went out in search of newer and yet newer loves. And this is the retribution of the soul for her unfaithful wanderings – that as separation grows greater she commences to know pain, and, becoming anxious therefrom to return to the source of her remembered joys, she finds herself unable to accomplish this because of the weight and grossness of the nature of the loves to which she has hired herself, and from which *she is totally unable to free herself*, and yet which she must by some means overcome that she may rise again to sanctity and return to God.

Now comes the marvellous, the pitiful, the universal Christ to her aid – the Mighty Lover; and we may see in the whole scheme of Creation, as we know it here, from jelly-fish to man, a plan by which the soul may bring her wanderings to a term in time conditions instead of timeless æons. When all this earth is evolved for her great need, at last by the mercy of God she is interned in the body of finite man, and must clothe herself in the heart and mind of the human and take upon herself the nature of this creature man, made and fashioned to be a suitable instrument and habitation for her. To counterbalance the grossness and ineptitude of the creature's material body with its appetites, man is imbued with the knowledge of right, and with a secret longing for *a happiness which is not that of the beast.*

The soul must raise the brute in him, with all its appetites, to purity, – a mighty task, accomplished with much pain, yet in infinitely shorter duration of pain than if left in disembodied spirit-life; and, indeed, we may come to look upon pain in this world as one of our best privileges because of its powers of purification within a time-limit, and to know that by the mercy of the God of Love we may take our hell of cleansing in this world rather than in those worlds of disembodied spirits where progress is of infinite slowness – revolving and revolving upon itself, as a sand-spiral in a blast-furnace, without hope of death.

Oh, how convey any warning of this terrible knowledge, which is not communicable by words! He said, 'Though one return from the dead, ye would not believe.' But, O soul! repent and return while still in the body! Lay hold on the Christ!

In the life of this world, then, does our God of love and mercy give us rapid means (by conquest of the animal grossness and corruptible body, raising man to the ideal man, according to God's intention) to reunite ourselves with Him. And the soul of all animal creation is also thereby gradually raised with us into a universal adoration of the One Almighty God.

This is no fallen but a rising world, in which all Creation is slowly and gloriously rising step by step.

So may our soul repay her debt to God for her past infidelities.

'Thy Maker is thine husband,' says the voice of the prophet.

And the creature, with its suffering heart and mind and body, has also its incomparable reward of bliss: for because of its love and obedience it is raised into the spiritual body, AND TOGETHER WITH THE SOUL BECOMES THE CHILD OF THE RESURRECTION.

.   .   .